YOUR KNOWLEDGE HAS VALUE

- We will publish your bachelor's and master's thesis, essays and papers

- Your own eBook and book - sold worldwide in all relevant shops

- Earn money with each sale

Upload your text at www.GRIN.com
and publish for free

Adam Balogh

Enabling Policies for Responding to "Hate Speech" in Practice

Responding to "Hate Speech" – Germany and Austria in comparison

GRIN Verlag

Bibliografische Information der Deutschen Nationalbibliothek:

Die Deutsche Bibliothek verzeichnet diese Publikation in der Deutschen National-
bibliografie; detaillierte bibliografische Daten sind im Internet über http://dnb.d-
nb.de/ abrufbar.

Dieses Werk sowie alle darin enthaltenen einzelnen Beiträge und Abbildungen
sind urheberrechtlich geschützt. Jede Verwertung, die nicht ausdrücklich vom
Urheberrechtsschutz zugelassen ist, bedarf der vorherigen Zustimmung des Verla-
ges. Das gilt insbesondere für Vervielfältigungen, Bearbeitungen, Übersetzungen,
Mikroverfilmungen, Auswertungen durch Datenbanken und für die Einspeicherung
und Verarbeitung in elektronische Systeme. Alle Rechte, auch die des auszugsweisen
Nachdrucks, der fotomechanischen Wiedergabe (einschließlich Mikrokopie) sowie
der Auswertung durch Datenbanken oder ähnliche Einrichtungen, vorbehalten.

Imprint:

Copyright © 2013 GRIN Verlag GmbH
Druck und Bindung: Books on Demand GmbH, Norderstedt Germany
ISBN: 978-3-656-37171-7

This book at GRIN:

http://www.grin.com/en/e-book/209230/enabling-policies-for-responding-to-hate-
speech-in-practice

GRIN - Your knowledge has value

Der GRIN Verlag publiziert seit 1998 wissenschaftliche Arbeiten von Studenten, Hochschullehrern und anderen Akademikern als eBook und gedrucktes Buch. Die Verlagswebsite www.grin.com ist die ideale Plattform zur Veröffentlichung von Hausarbeiten, Abschlussarbeiten, wissenschaftlichen Aufsätzen, Dissertationen und Fachbüchern.

Visit us on the internet:

http://www.grin.com/

http://www.facebook.com/grincom

http://www.twitter.com/grin_com

CENTRAL EUROPEAN UNIVERSITY

Enabling Policies for Responding to "Hate Speech" in Practice

Responding to "Hate Speech" – Germany and Austria in comparison

Adam Balogh

18/01/2013

Contents

1. Introduction 2
2. Legal responses to "Hate Speech" 4
3. Country comparison between Germany and Austria 7
   3.1. Germany 9
   3.2. Austria 10
4. Summary of the Real Life Response to „Hate Speech" 11
5. Policy Recommendations 13
6. Bibliography 14

1. Introduction

In 2004, the German physical education instructor Stefan Herre founded the Islamophobic and extreme right website "Politically Incorrect". What started as a small blog of an individual is today the largest German-speaking website for the extreme right and Islam enemies (Spiegel Online 2011). It is ranked among the thousand biggest German websites in terms of traffic and more than 60,000 people visit daily "Politically Incorrect". A large part of them come from Austria and Switzerland (Frankfurter Rundschau 2011).

Unfortunately, this example shows that even today, more than 60 years after fascism, Muslims often face hostility in both Germany and Austria. The so called "Hate Speech", and the institutionalization of "Hate Speech" by websites like "Politically Incorrect", account for a large part of this hostility. Therefore, the state, which has the responsibility of protecting its citizens, has also the duty to develop effective ways of responding to "Hate Speech". This term paper deals with the question whether Germany or Austria have these effective policies for responding to "Hate Speech". And if yes, which one of these two countries has better legal or extralegal ways for a response.

The reason why these two countries have been selected is simple: Firstly, in both countries German is the official language. Secondly, both countries have a very similar past, particularly in relation to National Socialism and the Second World War. Thirdly, they face the same challenge regarding immigration. In both countries the majority of immigrants come from Muslim countries. And fourthly, the results of a comparison are also more comparable when using the same source of "Hate Speech" in two different countries.

In order to answer these questions the procedure is as follows: At first, a very brief definition of so called "Hate Speech" and a summary of the ongoing debate among scholars whether laws against "Hate Speech" are a necessity for a democratic society or a slippery slope into censorship. After that, a detailed comparison will be made between Germany and Austria, where the focus is on the legal situation in these two states. What do the constitutions of both countries say regarding "Hate Speech" and the freedom of expression? What is the legal situation? Are there any "hate speech" laws? In order to illustrate this, a summary of the experiences in a real life test will be given. The question here is whether authorities in Germany and Austria are acting resolutely against "Hate Speech". For this purpose a "Real Life Response to „Hate Speech"" was initiated by all members of the CEU course "Enabling Policies for Responding to "Hate Speech" in Practice" and the results are summarized here. It should be noted that, this chapter is mostly a verbatim reproduction of the "Summary of the Real Life Response to "Hate Speech"" which was already handed in to the course instructor. At last a policy recommendation will be given which refers to the results of the legal and extralegal comparison in terms of "Hate Speech" in Germany and Austria.

2. Legal responses to "Hate Speech"

Before joining the debate whether banning the so called "Hate Speech" is a necessity for a democratic society or a slippery slope into censorship, a proper definition of "Hate Speech" is crucial. A very brief and proper definition of "Hate Speech" is: "Hate Speech is speech disparaging a racial, sexual, or ethnic group or a member of such a group." (Dictionary.com 2013). Here, the medium of such a "Hate Speech" doesn't matter. It may be a public speech of an individual, an entire book or just a single symbol as a swastika. The head and front of "Hate Speech" is that it offends the dignity of particular group of people (usually a minority).

In a free society, like Germany and Austria, all men are equal and one of the highest goals of the state is to enforce this equality through laws and actions. The problem here is that in this way other inalienable human rights such as freedom of expression can be restricted. Stephen Holmes sums it up quite well with the following sentences: *"The different values in play could be formulated, at the individual level, as individual freedom of expression versus personal dignity. Protecting the one or the other has social consequences; emphasizing the first enhances the legitimacy of the political system; emphasizing the second enhances the harmony of the society."* In addition, he refers to the importance of history and traditions in order to show how different states deal with this dilemma and writes: *"It does not take Sigmund Freud to understand that, if you have two continents, in one of which one hundred million people were killed on the basis of highly violent hate ideologies, accompanied and propelled by extreme hate speech, and in the other of which, at least by comparison, basically nothing happened, you will get different judicial traditions."* (Holmes 2012, 345-351). Holmes refers here to the U.S. and most European countries. While the U.S. has relatively loose "Hate Speech" laws and freedom of expression is traditionally inviolable, most European states go much more decisively against "Hate Speech" and even prohibit some statements such as Holocaust denial.

In the debate about the necessity of banning "Hate Speech", Holmes position is that any kind of restriction of freedom of expression is dangerous. In his opinion, *"We should be very worried not about (or at least not only about) the official, petty or high, who determines what orthodoxy we should speak, but about private groups getting a hold of this power to decide what can be said."* (Holmes 2012, 345-351).

Other scientists dealing with "Hate Speech" come to the same or alike conclusions. Peter Molnar warns that "Hate Speech" laws which prohibit communication based solely on its content can be always subject to the arbitrary judgment of the majority or the ruling group (Molnar 2012, 183-197). Ronald Dworkin goes even further than Molnar and claims that: *"Freedom for hate speech or group defamation is the price we pay for enforcing the laws that the haters and defamers oppose (for example, laws forbidding discrimination)."* In relation to democracy, Dworkin's opinion is that *"Fair democracy requires [...] that each citizen have not just a vote but a voice: a majority decision is not fair unless everyone has had a fair opportunity to express his or her attitudes or opinions or fears or tastes or presuppositions or prejudices or ideals, not just in the hope of influencing others (though that hope is crucially important), but also just to confirm his or her standing as a responsible agent in, rather than a passive victim of, collective action."* (Waldron 2012, 329-340). Professor Dworkin's conclusion is that while government must treat the fate of each citizen as of equal importance, individuals need not to do so (Dworkin 2012, 341-344).

While Peter Molnar is in the favor of art, education and the so called "Imminent Danger Test" to challenge "Hate Speech" (Molnar 2012, 183-197), Ronald Dworkin even rejects the last one (Dworkin 2012, 341-344). The "Imminent Danger Test" is a way to deal with "Hate Speech". Its principle is that states only should become active against even the worst forms of "Hate Speech" and discrimination, if a situation of imminent danger is given. Molnar writes on this: *"Art and education in the broadest sense, combined with a careful application of the "imminent danger" test, provide useful remedies against "hate speech" in all democracies. One of these two responses should help in all situations. If expressions create a clear and present danger of violent action, they can be banned under the "imminent danger" test."* Further Molnar justifies his opinion as follows: *"[...] creative artistic and other educational responses to expressions, including art and symbolic speech, that can be labeled "hate speech" are much more effective than content-based laws, and do not put freedom of speech at risk in the way legal restrictions on public communication do."* (Molnar 2012, 183-197).

But there are also scientists, like Jeremy Waldron, who claims that banning "Hate Speech" is necessary in free society. In Waldron's opinion Dworkin exaggerates the role of legitimacy. Referring to this, Waldron writes: *"There is no doubt that Dworkin has drawn attention to a troubling consequence of legislation forbidding hate speech. But how serious are these consequences? It is difficult to tell because "legitimacy" is a vague term, and there is a question about what "spoiling" the legitimacy of these laws actually amounts to. In social science, legitimacy often involves little more than the fact of popular support."* Further he claims that there is only a very loose connection between "Hate Speech" laws and political legitimacy and that "Hate Speech" laws could have a beneficial chilling effect on everyone's speech (Waldron 2012, 329-340).

3. Country comparison between Germany and Austria

The previous chapter showed the different pros and cons of banning "Hate Speech". This chapter will deal with a detailed comparison between Germany and Austria. The focus is on the legal situation in these two states, but this chapter starts with international laws and agreements against "Hate Speech", that affect these two states.

Germany and Austria, both countries, are members of the Council of Europe. It therefore affects both states that the European Council has decided to foster new strategies to counter "Hate Speech." Tarlach Mc Gonagle writes that this new strategy includes three main points: *"Firstly, the prevention, prohibition and punishment of certain types of expression. Secondly, the facilitation and creation of expressive and communicative opportunities for minorities. And thirdly, the promotion of tolerance, understanding, and intergroup and intercultural dialogue."* (Mc Gonagle 2012, 456-498).

In their decision to challenge "Hate Speech", the Council of Europe refers to the international treaty of the European Convention of Human Rights (ECHR). Germany and Austria, both, signed this treaty. Here, especially Articles 10 and 17 of the ECHR and the interplay between them are the ground for actions against "Hate Speech" (Mc Gonagle 2012, 456-498). Article 10 of the ECHR provides the right to freedom of expression, but also set its restrictions (e.g. "Hate Speech"). Article 17 ECHR even underlines this and provides that no one may use the rights guaranteed by the ECHR to seek the abolition or limitation of rights guaranteed in the Convention.

The International Covenant on Civil and Political Rights (ICCPR) is also signed and ratified by Germany and Austria and Toby Mendel claims that: *"[...] (it) does indeed provide sensible standards, at least in relation to criminal prohibitions on "Hate Speech", and that these standards are precise and coherent."* Further Mendel writes that especially article 19 and 20 ICCPR are important. Article 19 ICCPR guarantees the right of freedom of expression and article 20 ICCPR requires states to prohibit "advocacy of national, racial or religious hatred that constitutes incitement to discrimination, hostility or violence." (Mendel 2012, 417-429).

Since 2007, the European Union is also challenging "Hate Speech" with its Council Framework Decision 2008/913/JHA. Germany and Austria are both members of the European Union and are also here affected. The decision combats certain forms and expressions of racism and xenophobia by means of criminal law (European Parliament Legislative Observatory 2013). After summarizing international laws and agreements against "Hate Speech", the next chapters will focus in detail on German and Austrian law.

3.1. Germany

The Basic Law for the Federal Republic of Germany (Grundgesetz) guarantees in article 5 the freedom of expression. However, the Federal Constitutional Court of Germany decided already in 1958 that it is in harmony with the Basic Law to limit this right in order to guarantee the first and most important article of the Basic Law, the human dignity (BVerfGE 7, 1 BvR 400/51). Therefore the German Parliament already decided in 1959 to pass a bill against incitement to hatred. Today, section 130 is still in the German criminal code and calls for punishment for Holocaust denial and incitement to hatred. Article 1 of section 130 German criminal code says that: *"Whosoever, in a manner capable of disturbing the public peace incites hatred against segments of the population or calls for violent or arbitrary measures against them; or assaults the human dignity of others by insulting, maliciously maligning, or defaming segments of the population, shall be liable to imprisonment from three months to five years."* Article 4 of section 130 German criminal code penalizes inter alia Holocaust denial and says: *"Whosoever publicly or in a meeting approves of, denies or downplays an act committed under the rule of National Socialism of the kind indicated in section 6 (1) of the Code of International Criminal Law, in a manner capable of disturbing the public peace shall be liable to imprisonment not exceeding five years or a fine."*

3.2. Austria

Like Germany, Austria has also far reaching laws against incitement to hatred and the glorification of National Socialism. Although freedom of expression is not in included in the Constitution of Austria, article 10 ECHR has constitutional status in Austria. But as mentioned before, article 10 of the ECHR provides not only the right to freedom of expression, but also set its restrictions (e.g. "Hate Speech"). Article 283 of the Austrian criminal code is such a restriction and calls for punishment for incitement to hatred. Its content is very similar to section 130 in the German criminal code and is also linked to human dignity. But Austria has also a second law, called "Prohibition act" (Verbotsgesetz), which bans every kind of Nazi organization, activity, glorification of National Socialism and Holocaust denial.

4. Summary of the Real Life Response to „Hate Speech"

While the previous chapter has dealt with the legal situation in Germany and Austria, this chapter focusses on the reactions of state authorities to a real life response to "Hate Speech". The response was addressed to the relevant competent authorities for protection against extremism. In both countries, this is the Ministry of the Interior. Heads of agencies in each case is the minister of the interior. On the basis of effectiveness, the ministers of the interior were contacted. In Germany, the minister of the interior is Hans-Peter Friedrich and in Austria Johanna Mikl-Leitner. An email was written to both, containing following questions:

1. Do you know the website "Politically Incorrect"?
2. What position do you represent with respect to this website?
3. Do you think the website meets the offense of sedition?
4. Do you think the website is a potential threat to public safety?
5. What can I as a German citizen do against this website?
6. Are you willing to support me in my actions against this website?

Unfortunately, Johanna Mikl-Leitner, the Austrian minister of the interior, did not reply to this Email, although a confirmation of receipt was received. Hans-Peter Friedrich, the German minister of the interior, however, has responded in a very long and detailed email. Unfortunately, his reply was of useless content: First of all, he did not write the answer himself, it was a clerk in his name. Secondly, although he knows the website and deplores it, he claims that it is not in his competence to deal with this problem. He writes that it is the competence of the Bundesamt für Verfassungsschutz (Secret Service to protect the Constitution) to deal with this problem. This is remarkable because the Bundesamt für Verfassungsschutz is under the control of the Ministry of the Interior and therefore to an extinct under the control of Hans-Peter Friedrich (Bundesamt für

Verfassungsschutz 2013). Further he writes that there is no possibility to cooperate with him. Instead I should report it to the police and take my problems with "Politically Incorrect" to a court.

Since no help was to be expected from the heads of the authorities, in a second step the same Email has been sent directly to the ministries. Unfortunately, in Germany this was simply not possible. The only way to get in contact with the ministry of the interior is to write them a very short message of 1000 letters (!) on their homepage (Bundesministerium des Inneren 2013). There is no Email address on the website and 1000 letters are way too short to explain them the concerns. In Austria, things were quite different. A kindly reply was received in which one was asked to send the questions to the dedicated "Meldestelle für NS-Wiederbetätigung" (hotline for Nazi re-operation). The Email was sending to the "Meldestelle für NS-Wiederbetätigung" but unfortunately, also in Austria the second step led to a letdown: Although the hotline for Nazi re-operation answered that they know the website and already watch their activities and their glad about any kind of information that supports their observation, there isn't the possibility of any further cooperation.

In conclusion it can be said that the authorities were more cooperative in Austria. But cooperation or any kind of action that contains more than just observing the website "Politically Incorrect" was not possible. So from an extralegal point of view both countries have failed in this concern, although Austria has at least a hotline for Nazi re-operation.

5. **Policy Recommendations**

The results of the Real Life Response to "Hate Speech" showed that in Germany and Austria a huge gap between written laws and reality exists. Although both states established comprehensive laws to challenge "Hate Speech", the real life test showed that an execution lags of willing. The Austrian hotline for Nazi re-operation is a step in the right direction but still not enough. The following policy recommendations may lead to improved results:

- The German and the Austrian Parliament should have a comprehensive debate about the pros and cons of banning "Hate Speech". If they decide to challenge "Hate Speech" via law, an adequate execution is necessary.
- Germany should also establish a hotline for Nazi re-operation. This hotline should not just collect information but also bring an action. This institution could serve as a preparer of class actions.
- People bringing actions against "Hate Speech" need a comprehensive financial relief in order to avoid chilling effects due to high legal costs.

6. Bibliography

Bundesamt für Verfassungsschutz. 2013. *Kontrolliert wie kaum eine andere Behörde.* http://alturl.com/2ndhm, Accessed on 09.01.2013.

Bundesministerium des Inneren. 2013. *Kontaktformular Bürgerservice.* http://alturl.com/h5n3e, Accessed on 09.01.2013.

Bundesverfassungsgericht. 1958. Urteil des Ersten Senats vom 15. Januar 1958. 1 BvR 400/51. http://alturl.com/q7xid [Lüth].

Dictionary.com. 2013. *Hate speech.* http://alturl.com/fsxkv, Accessed on 17.01.2013.

Dworkin, Ronald. 2012. "Reply to Jeremy Waldron." In Michael Herz/Peter Molnar (Ed.). *The Content and Context of Hate Speech. Rethinking Regulation and Responses.* Cambridge: Cambridge University Press: 342-344.

European Parliament Legislative Observatory. 2013. *2001/0270(CNS) - 28/11/2008 Final act.* http://alturl.com/obubh, Accessed on 18.01.2013.

Frankfurter Rundschau. 2011. *Im Netz der Islamfeinde.* http://alturl.com/qtkv7, Accessed on 09.01.2013.

Mc Gonagle, Tarlach. 2012. "A Survey and Critical Analysis of Council of Europe Strategies for Countering "Hate Speech"." In Michael Herz/Peter Molnar (Ed.). *The Content and Context of Hate Speech. Rethinking Regulation and Responses.* Cambridge: Cambridge University Press: 456-498.

Mendel, Toby. 2012. "Does International Law Provide For Consistent Rules on Hate Speech?" In Michael Herz/Peter Molnar (Ed.). *The Content and Context of Hate Speech. Rethinking Regulation and Responses.* Cambridge: Cambridge University Press: 417-429.

Molnar, Peter. 2012. "Responding to "Hate Speech" With Art, Education, and the Imminent-Danger Test." In Michael Herz/Peter Molnar (Ed.). *The Content and Context of Hate Speech. Rethinking Regulation and Responses.* Cambridge: Cambridge University Press: 183-197.

Holmes, Stephen. 2012. „Waldron, Machiavelli, and Hate Speech." In Michael Herz/Peter Molnar (Ed.). *The Content and Context of Hate Speech. Rethinking Regulation and Responses.* Cambridge: Cambridge University Press: 345-351.

Spiegel Online. 2011. *"Politically Incorrect" eng vernetzt mit rechter Szene.* http://alturl.com/iokzw, Accessed on 09.01.2013.

Waldron, Jeremy. 2012. "Hate Speech and Political Legitimacy." In Michael Herz/Peter Molnar (Ed.). *The Content and Context of Hate Speech. Rethinking Regulation and Responses.* Cambridge: Cambridge University Press: 329-340.